How do they work?

Toys with Springs

Wendy Sadler

Heinemann Library
Chicago, Illinois

Editorial: Andrew Farrow and Dan Nunn
Design: Ron Kamen and Dave Oakley/Arnos Design
Picture Research: Hannah Taylor
Production: Duncan Gilbert

Originated by Ambassador Litho Ltd
Printed and bound in China by South China Printing Company.

09 08 07 06 05
10 9 8 7 6 5 4 3 2 1

Library of Congress Cataloging-in-Publication Data
Sadler, Wendy.
  How do they work? : toys with springs / Wendy Sadler.
     p. cm.
  Includes bibliographical references and index.
  ISBN 1-4034-6829-X (hc. : library binding) -- ISBN 1-4034-6835-4 (pbk.)
  1. Mechanical toys. I. Title: Toys with springs. II. Title.
  TS2301.T7S25 2005
  688.7'28--dc22
                                        2004020663

Acknowledgements
The publishers would like to thank the following for permission to reproduce photographs:
Alamy Images (Elmtree Images) p. **27**; Harcourt Education Ltd (Christine Martin) p. **21**; Harcourt Education Ltd (Tudor Photography) pp. **4**, **5**, **6** (top and bottom), **7**, **8**, **9**, **10**, **11**, **12**, **13**, **14**, **15**, **16**, **17**, **18**, **19**, **20**, **22**, **23**, **24**, **25**, **26**, **28**, **29**.

Cover photograph reproduced with permission of Harcourt Education Ltd (Tudor Photography).

Every effort has been made to contact copyright holders of any material reproduced in this book. Any omissions will be rectified in subsequent printings if notice is given to the publishers.

The paper used to print this book comes from sustainable resources.

Contents

Some words are shown in bold, **like this**. You can find out what they mean by looking in the glossary.

Toys with Springs

Lots of toys have springs. Springs can make toys move. Some toys have springs inside them. Other toys have springs on the outside.

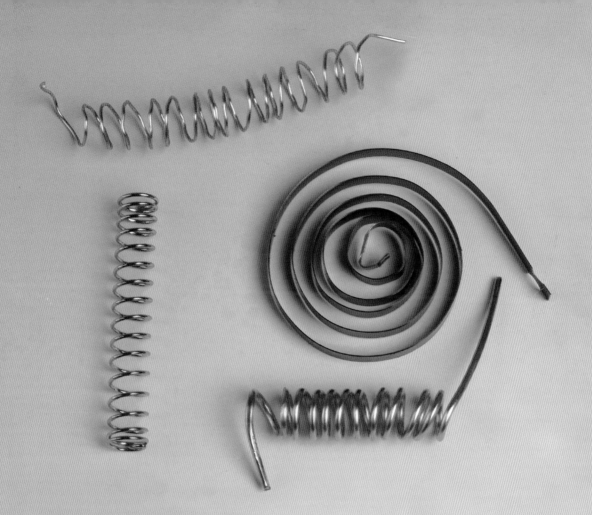

Springs come in many shapes and sizes. A spring can be pushed or pulled to change its shape. When you let go, the spring goes back to the shape it was before.

What Is a Spring?

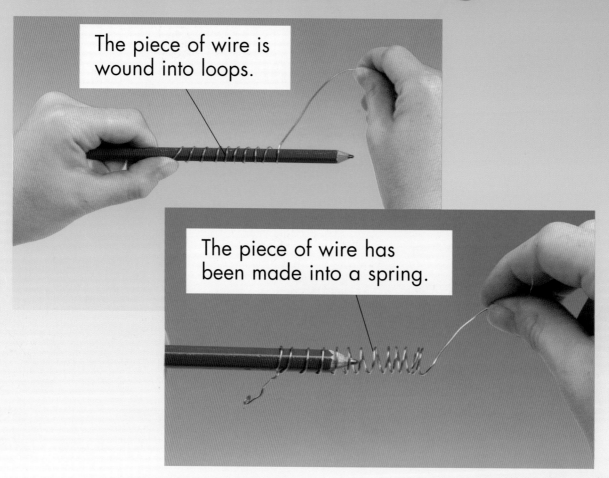

The piece of wire is wound into loops.

The piece of wire has been made into a spring.

A spring is made from a long piece of **metal** or **plastic**. The metal or plastic is shaped into lots of loops. You can make a spring by wrapping a piece of wire around a pencil.

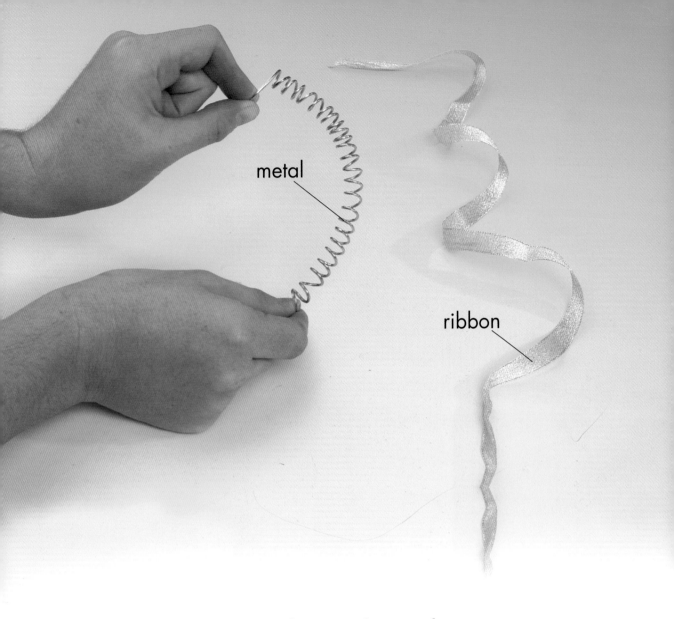

metal

ribbon

Springs are made of metal or plastic because these **materials** stay in loops. A spring made of ribbon or string would not work!

Squashing a Spring

Springs can be pushed so they get shorter. When you push a spring, it feels like it is pushing you back. The spring tries to get back to the shape and size it was before you pushed it.

The spring pushes back.

You can push a spring to make it shorter.

This spring has gone back to its normal shape after being let go.

You use your **energy** to **squash** a spring and make it shorter. The spring holds your energy until you let it go. When you let go, the spring uses the energy to **stretch** back into shape.

9

Stretching a Spring

The spring
pulls back.

You pull a spring
to make it longer.

When you pull a spring you **stretch** it
and make it longer. It feels like the spring
is pulling you back. When you let go, the
spring moves back into shape.

This spring has been
stretched too far.

If you pull a spring too far it will not go
back to the shape it was before. The
spring stops being springy!

Jack-in-the-Box

Inside this box is a puppet on a spring. The spring is **squashed** down so it fits inside the box.

When the box lid is opened, the squashed spring inside jumps back into shape. The puppet on the end of the spring jumps out of the box.

The spring is hidden under the puppet's clothes.

Jumping Springs

This toy has a spring and a **plastic** cup.
By **squashing** the spring you can make
the cup stick to the bottom of the toy.
This stores **energy** inside the spring.

plastic cup

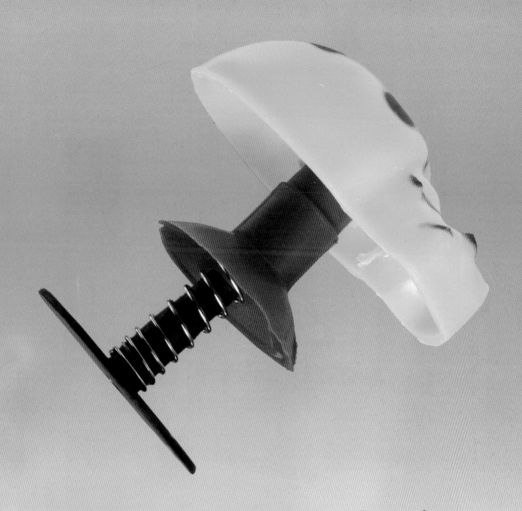

The spring tries to **stretch** back to the shape it was at the start. After a short time it pushes the cup away from the bottom of the toy. It does this with so much energy that the toy flies into the air.

15

Springs That Launch Things

This toy uses a spring to fire a ping-pong ball into the air. When you push down the button, the spring is **squashed**. When you let go of the button, the spring **stretches** out and **launches** the ball.

spring

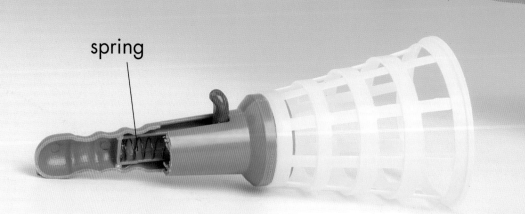

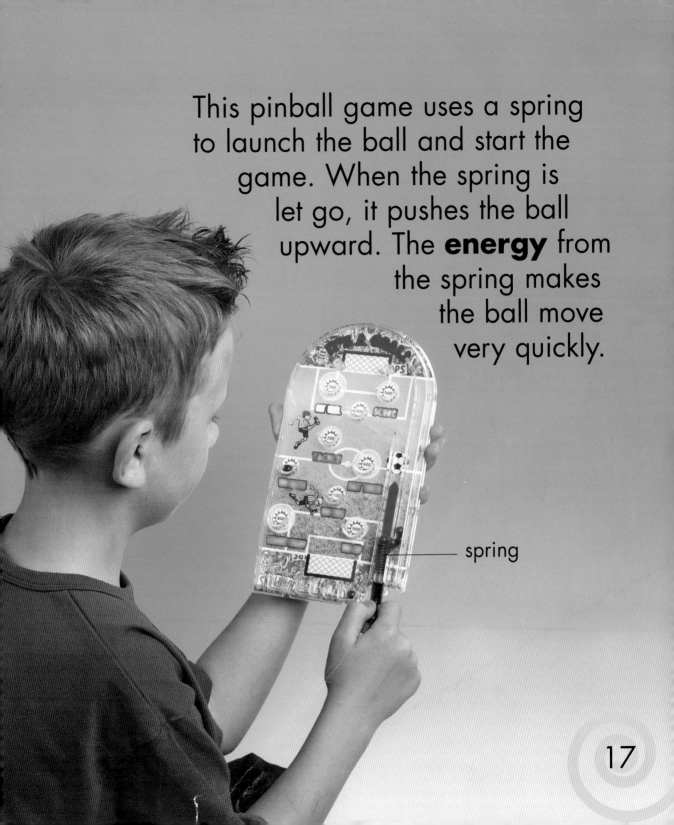

This pinball game uses a spring to launch the ball and start the game. When the spring is let go, it pushes the ball upward. The **energy** from the spring makes the ball move very quickly.

spring

17

Bouncing on Springs

pull

This toy hangs from a spring. If you pull the toy down you **stretch** out the spring. This makes the spring bigger than it was before.

The spring
squashes up.

The toy bounces
up and down.

When the toy is pulled
down, the spring wants
to go back to the shape it
was before. It jumps back
so fast that it **squashes**
up. This makes the toy
bounce up and down.

Sitting on Springs

Springs can make playing more fun. This ride has a seat on top of a giant spring. You can bounce around on it.

This bicycle has springs under the seat. The springs **cushion** the bumps in the road. This means you do not feel all the bumps. Your ride is more **comfortable**.

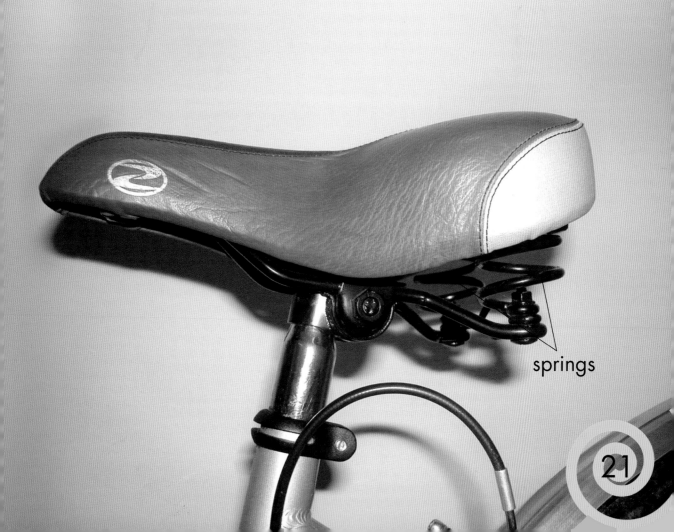

springs

Long Springs

This very long spring can be **stretched** out even longer. If you let go of a spring like this at the top of the stairs, it will climb down.

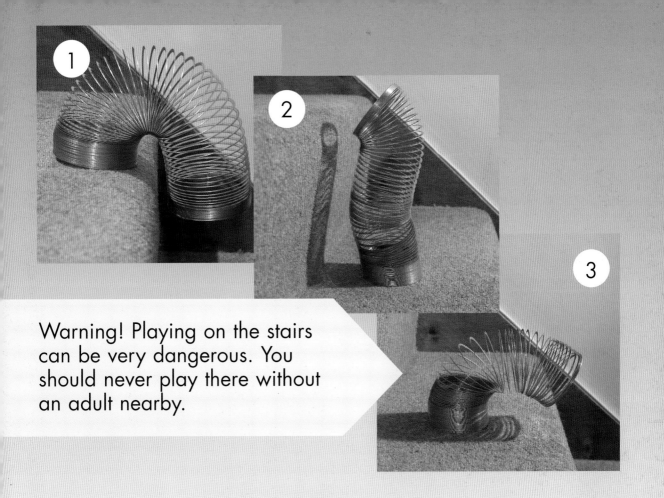

1

2

3

Warning! Playing on the stairs can be very dangerous. You should never play there without an adult nearby.

The spring stretches out as it falls down the first step. The back part of the spring is pulled down on to the second step. Next, the spring stretches again until it begins to fall down the third step. Soon it will have fallen all the way down the stairs!

Springs Inside Toys

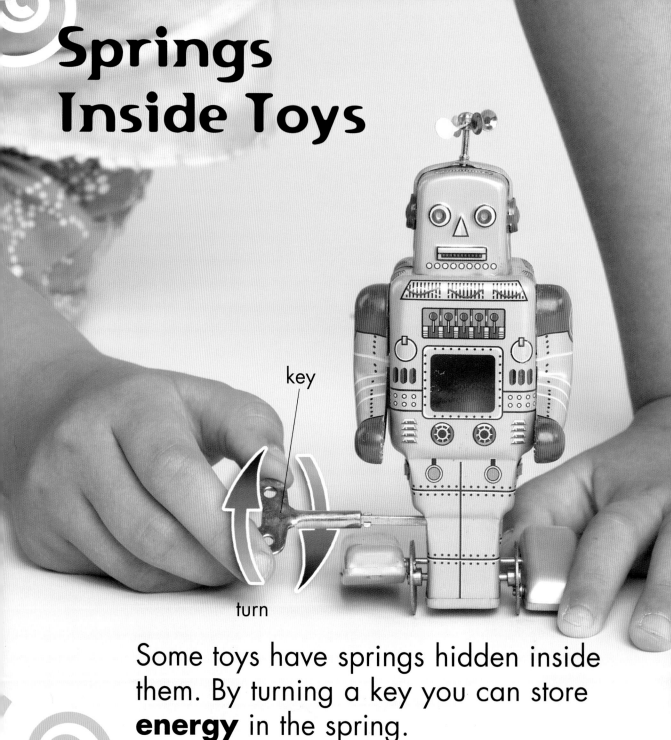

key

turn

Some toys have springs hidden inside them. By turning a key you can store **energy** in the spring.

As the spring inside this toy robot moves back into shape, it makes the feet of the robot move. The robot looks like it is walking.

Windup Spring Toys

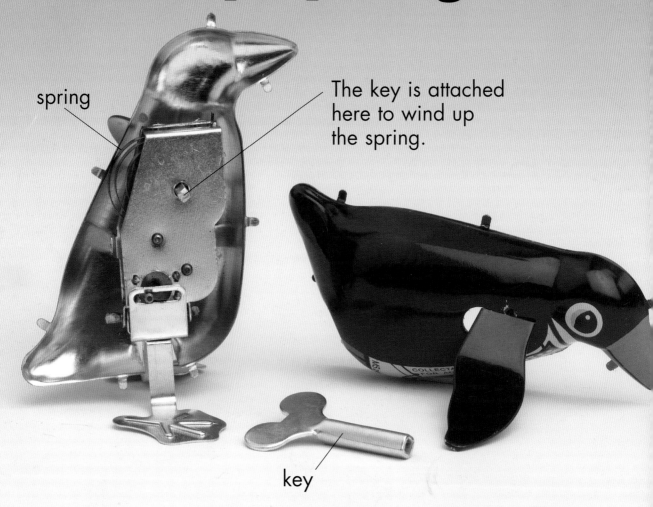

spring

The key is attached
here to wind up
the spring.

key

This penguin is a windup toy. When you
turn the key, you **squash** the spring inside.
The spring then tries to go back to the
shape it was before. This moves the toy.

spring

Old clocks and watches used to work using springs like this. That is why windup toys are sometimes called clockwork toys.

Having Fun with Springs

Springs can be lots of fun to play with. They can jump in the air, bounce up and down, and even walk down stairs!

Some toys use springs to fire things in the air.

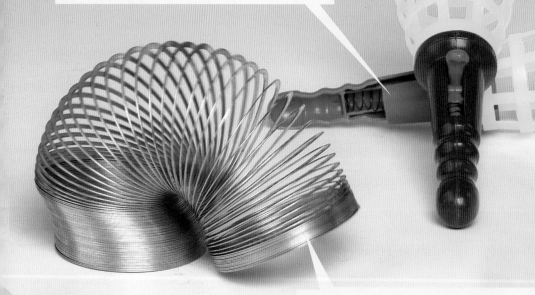

Long springs can move around like a slinky snake.

Springs can pop up and give you a surprise.

Windup toys can move around using the **energy** in a spring.

Glossary

comfortable not painful

cushion make something feel softer or
   less painful

energy something that is used to make
   things move

launch make something fly up into the air

material something that is used to
   make things.

metal hard, shiny material. Knives and
   forks are often made of metal.

plastic strong, light material that can be
   made in lots of different shapes

squash crush or squeeze something

stretch when something gets longer

More Books to Read

Glover, David. *What Do Springs Do?* Chicago: Heinemann Library, 1997.

Green, Joey. *The Official Slinky Book: Hundreds of Wild and Wacky Uses for the Greatest Toy on Earth.* New York: Berkley Publishing Group, 1999.

Royston, Angela. *Bendy and Rigid.* Chicago: Heinemann Library, 2003.

Index